What To do

When You're Angry with God

By

Rev. Mrs. Jimmy Gee

Preface

Today, this book is for those that, after being honest with themselves, have to accept the fact that they are angry with God. This book will not condemn you or make you feel guilty. Instead, it will help you see from a different perspective. After reading this book, I pray your relationship with the Lord Jesus Christ grows stronger. I pray that, after reading this book, you understand that anger is often rooted in fear, yet God does not give us a spirit of fear! I love you deeply, and thank you sincerely for taking the time to read my book.

Copyright © 2025 Mrs. Jimmy Gee All rights reserved

The characters and events portrayed in this book are fictitious. Any similarity to real persons, living or dead, is coincidental and not intended by the author.

No part of this book may be reproduced, or stored in a retrieval system, or transmitted in any form or by any means, electronic, mechanical, photocopying, recording, or otherwise, without express written permission of the publisher.

Printed in the United States of America

Table of Contents

Preface 2

Chapter 1 Dealing with Shame 5

Chapter 2 Be Careful 7

Chapter 3 It's Not All About You 9

Chapter 4 Don't Leave! 11

Chapter 5 Childhood Sexual Abuse 20

Chapter 6 Tell God How You Feel 24

Chapter 7 Real vs Lukewarm 27

Chapter 8 The Consequences 30

Chapter 9 God is NOT Your Personal Genie 34

Chapter 10 Don't be Weak! 38

Chapter 11 The Bottom Line 41

Chapter 12 Stay Focused 44

Chapter 1 Dealing with Shame

Many people walk through life unaware that their behavior, decisions, and even lifestyle choices are influenced by being angry with God. The first step to healing from any issue is admitting exactly how you feel. You are not a horrible person for admitting that you are angry.

Anger is an emotion we all feel; however, there is often a sense of shame associated with being angry at God. The reason there is shame is that we secretly believe God is someone we should worship but never feel anger toward. While that may be true and we will dig deeper into that, it is very important that you actually admit that you feel this way.

Understand that feelings of shame and guilt are not Godly emotions; they are demonic. Emotions that are demonic include jealousy, anger, fear, guilt, and shame. God does not want us to live in those emotions.

With that being said, you may have been making decisions throughout your life that reflect a person angry with God, and some people have not taken the time to sit with themselves and process their emotions enough to realize that God is the one they're upset with.

Many people think they're angry with their circumstances or with those who abused or hurt them, but ultimately, many are angry with God. There are people who have been sexually abused, people who have been hurt by others in the Church, and those harmed by individuals who called themselves prophets. Often, people associate those individuals with God and the problem with that is, instead of forgiving those people, they cut God out of their life.

They cut Him out by stopping Church attendance, ceasing to read their Bible, fasting less, and drifting away from their faith. It is extremely important that you admit you feel this way. Admitting your feelings allows you to open your heart and allow God to work in your life in ways you never imagined.

Own your emotions! There is nothing you can say to God that He cannot handle. Nothing you have experienced is beyond what God has seen or can redeem.

Chapter 2 Be Careful

It is important to understand that narcissists are often created from trauma. From a spiritual standpoint, narcissism begins with pain that turns into bitterness and eventually becomes a spirit of self-centeredness one that is opportunistic, self-serving, and focused only on personal gain rather than on the good of others.

Even when a narcissist performs good deeds, those deeds are usually done for self-gratification, to boost their ego, or to gain attention.

The reason I say *be careful not to become a narcissist* is because when you allow your anger toward God to take over, it begins to shift your way of thinking. You move away from a Christian mindset and begin channeling vengeful, resentful, and selfish thoughts, things that only come from demonic forces.

To say, "I'm angry with Church people, so I'm not going to Church anymore," or "I'm angry with God, so I'll stop reading my Bible," is dangerous thinking. If you are no longer worshiping God or living a Christian lifestyle, then the question must be asked: **Who are you serving?**

Who do you turn to when times become difficult?
Who do you pray to when you are in pain?
Who do you call upon when things are not going your way?

It becomes narcissistic because narcissists believe they can solve all of their own problems. They manipulate people the way chess players move their pieces using others for personal advantage without caring about how it affects anyone else. Every narcissist is driven by internal bitterness.

Please, do not let that become you. Do not become so angry with God that you become angry with the world as well. Do not remove God's protection from your life because you stopped serving Him simply because He didn't answer your prayers as quickly as you wanted Him to.

You will see this throughout the book:
God is not your personal genie.
God is not your DJ, waiting to play whatever song you request so you can move through life however you please.

God is a God of unconditional love and forgiveness. He is not the originator of *transactional relationships.* A transactional relationship says, "Because I gave you something, I expect something in return." That is not how God works.

If you are serving God only because you want something from Him, it's no different than a person performing kind gestures just to get something back.

Think about how you would feel if you found out someone in your life was only nice to you because they benefited from it. You would be hurt and rightfully so.

If we wouldn't accept that kind of behavior from others, why should God accept it from us?

Chapter 3 It's Not All About You

The reason I titled this chapter *It's Not All About You* is because we must understand that when God makes decisions, He is not thinking solely about us. He is also thinking about the people around us.

Your gain could be someone else's loss.

Let me give you an example: imagine I am house shopping, driving through different neighborhoods, looking at homes and deciding where I'd like to live. As I drive, I spot one house I absolutely fall in love with and decide I want it. Suppose I end up getting that house, wonderful for me but I must also remember that someone else used to live there.

What about them?

Another example: I may want a specific job and eventually get it. But the reality is, someone else had that position before me. When I got the job, they lost theirs.

It's not all about you. Sometimes, when God tells you *no,* He is protecting others, just as He protects you.

The same way God considers your best interests, He considers the best interests of others. Just as He may tell someone else *"no"* because that choice could harm your life, He may tell *you* no because it could negatively affect someone else's.

God is not only thinking of you. He is also protecting others whose paths cross with yours.

So, when you pray for certain things, remember this: your requests might affect someone else's life in ways you cannot see. Sometimes, God's "no" is not a rejection, it's a redirection rooted in compassion.

When we talk to God and ask Him for the things we believe we want, we should do so with humanity, compassion, and consideration for others in mind.

It is not all about you. You are not the only person on the planet. Just as your loss could be someone else's gain, your gain might mean someone else's loss. God's plan accounts for every life connected to yours.

Chapter 4 Don't Leave!

There are many reasons a person can become angry with God. Sometimes people are angry because they can't understand why God allowed certain things to happen to them. Others are angry because they don't understand how God could allow certain people to enter their lives and hurt them. Some are angry because they believe God should have protected them and He didn't.

Some people become angry when they see those who have hurt them prosper in life. Others are angry because they feel stuck, as if they keep taking five steps forward only to fall eight steps back. Some are angry because they feel they've done everything right, yet God still hasn't answered their prayers.

Let me give you an example.

A man once posted on social media:

"Sixty years of being a Christian, and I have never had a healthy relationship. I hate my job. I've been diagnosed with cancer. I tithe every Sunday, and now I can't afford to retire. So much for being a Christian!"

Many people feel the same way but let's examine this carefully.

If you're angry because you feel God allowed something painful to happen, I want to remind you that sometimes God truly *does* allow us to go through certain experiences to make us stronger. Other times, however, we suffer because of choices we made ourselves.

If you are bitter because you dated someone who ruined your life and now blame God for "allowing it," consider that perhaps God never instructed you to be with that person in the first place.

Most of life's major decisions relationships, career choices, friendships should be made prayerfully, with fasting, study, and patience.

Fasting isn't just a spiritual trend or a ritual for when we want something from God. Fasting is a way to draw closer to Him, to hear His voice and receive clarity. Many of us make impulsive decisions without praying or fasting first. Then, when things fall apart, we blame God.

But God didn't tell you to do those things.
He didn't tell you to enter that relationship.
He didn't tell you to start using substances.
He didn't tell you to join ungodly friendships or live in sin.
And He never told you to have premarital sex.

So when you find yourself in a relationship that begins beautifully but ends in heartbreak don't blame God. You have to take accountability for the choices you made outside His will.

Every major life decision should begin with prayer, fasting, and quiet time with God. You should have a space in your home dedicated solely to prayer. Fasting should not just be from food, but also from worldly distractions, ungodly content, gossip, and the things that weaken your spirit.

How dare we live ungodly lives and then expect God to bless us? How can we expect Him to overlook the wrongs we repeatedly commit just because we sprinkle in small moments of "Christianity" going to Church, giving 10%, or praying occasionally while continuing to watch ungodly things, curse, gossip, drink, and live without obedience?

Inconsistency is disrespectful to God.

Now, for those who are angry because they've suffered abuse, physical, emotional, or sexual, please understand this truth: **God did not do that to you.**

Sometimes, we endure such trauma so that our story can become a testimony a light that helps others heal.

I can say this from experience. I have been molested. I have been raped. I have been physically abused. Some of those experiences even came from people within the Church. There was a period when I was deeply angry with God, disgusted by the idea of living a Christian life because I couldn't see beyond my pain.

But as I grew spiritually, I began to understand that God calls us to be *slow to anger.* He showed me that for every person who wrongs you, He will deal with them far more justly and powerfully than you ever could.

I am not boasting when I say this, but many of those who wronged me are not doing well. They are living under God's judgment.

I had to release my anger and realize: **God fights harder than I ever could.**

When I chose to forgive, it was like taking a hundred-pound weight off my back. Forgiveness didn't excuse what happened it freed me.

Once I began to forgive and pray for those who hurt me, my story became a source of healing for others.

Sexual abuse is not just physical trauma it's spiritual, emotional, and deeply psychological. It can make you question your identity and sexual identity, your worth, even your faith. But God is strong enough to heal all of that.

Instead of allowing tragedy to turn me into a victim, I let it shape my Ministry. I began to lead workshops, speak at events, coach others, and write books that teach people how to overcome pain.

Blaming God keeps you trapped in a victim mindset. And you are not a victim, you are a **survivor.**

Some people are angry with God because they see their enemies doing better than them. They watch the people who hurt them living comfortably traveling, making money, eating fine food, raising healthy children, and climbing the ladder of success.

But what you must understand is this: **what you see isn't always what's real.**

Stop looking at social media as proof of people's happiness. Stop comparing your life to others'. Even if you see them daily, remember people who live outside of Christ are often living under deception.

When someone rejects God, they step into a demonic space. There is no gray area between light and darkness.

And one of the devil's most dangerous tactics is deception through abundance. The devil will gladly give you anything your heart desires but in exchange for your soul.

Look at much of Hollywood today. Not all, but many celebrities live glamorous lives full of beauty, fame, and wealth. They have private jets, luxury brands, and status but many have traded peace for possessions.

Even some pastors fall into this trap. Wearing crosses and preaching eloquently doesn't guarantee salvation. Some preach powerful sermons on Sunday yet live in sin Monday through Saturday. They wear $10,000 suits, drive luxury cars, and boast about blessings while their congregation waits at the bus stop.

Wearing a cross doesn't make you saved.

We must not envy people who seem to prosper in sin. Their success is temporary. The devil gives quickly but he collects painfully.

He knows his fate. He knows he will never see heaven again. That's why his goal is to drag as many souls as possible with him. Don't let yours be one of them.

Even if others seem to be winning while you struggle, remember this: *God's timing is perfect.* Some people won't face judgment until later. Your job is not to worry about when, your job is to trust God's justice.

Faith means believing God will provide what you need, even when others seem to have more. Many of those "blessed" people you see are drowning in debt or emotional misery. Their lives may look full, but their souls are empty.

Jesus didn't walk the earth covered in gold. While there's nothing wrong with having nice things, we must never worship them.

If your anger toward God is rooted in not having material possessions, then you're worshiping idols, not God. As Christians, we do not worship idols or false gods.

Some people are angry because they feel stuck as if their life hasn't progressed in years. They've tried, prayed, and pushed, but nothing seems to change.

What they don't realize is that sometimes blessings come later in life. Many successful people musicians, writers, entrepreneurs didn't find success until they had fallen flat on their faces multiple times.

Delay is not denial.

You might be asking God for something He's intentionally withholding because it could destroy you.

Let me share a personal story.

Twenty years ago, I desperately wanted to work at a famous company. I applied repeatedly but was always rejected. I was frustrated, because working there would have looked incredible on my résumé.

After two decades, I finally got hired. My name was on the door, my photo on the website I was proud. But soon, I realized the job was one of the most toxic environments I had ever worked in. It became so bad I had to seek legal counsel.

Only then did I understand: when God said "no" years earlier, He was **protecting** me.

We think we know what's best for us but we can't see the road ahead. God can.

His "no" is often His mercy.

When people become bitter with God, they often look elsewhere for control turning to the occult, witchcraft, and false spirituality.

This is dangerous.

I'm not referring to people raised in non-Christian traditions; I'm speaking to those who once knew Christ but turned away because they were angry or impatient.

Many begin experimenting with incense, herbs, spells, or ancestor altars to get the things God already said *no* to.

What they don't realize is that while witchcraft may appear to work for a season, it removes God's protection.

Psychic powers may seem real. Dreams may come true. Spells may "manifest" results. But behind all of it are demons masquerading as light.

Those spirits will eventually turn on you. Many who toyed with witchcraft lost their minds, their families, or even their lives when the same demons they invited demanded repayment.

You don't have to place offerings before altars because God already gave the ultimate sacrifice: His Son.

Sometimes God delays your blessing for 20, 30, or even 50 years not because He's forgotten you, but because you weren't ready until now.

Many things we think we're ready for would destroy us if we received them too soon.

To the man who said, "I've been faithful for 60 years and now I'm sick, broke, and alone," I say this:

How do you know God won't use your healing to inspire someone else's faith?
How do you know your cancer won't go into remission through prayer, fasting, and discipline becoming the very miracle that brings others to Christ?

Your story could become someone else's testimony.

That's why I say again: **It's not all about you.**

Sometimes the delay, the pain, and the unanswered prayers aren't punishments they're assignments.

When life feels unfair, read the story of Job. Job lost everything his children, his wealth, his health. Even his wife told him to curse God. But Job refused. His faith never wavered.

And in time, God restored everything and gave him twice as much as before.

The story of Job reminds us: faith is proven not when life is good, but when everything falls apart.

Anyone can love God when life is easy. True faith is loving Him when life hurts.

When life rises, praise God.
When life falls, praise Him even louder.

Because turning away from God when you're angry doesn't punish Him it only removes His protection from you.

And when God's covering is gone, the enemy moves in.

Don't leave.

Stay anchored.
Stay faithful.
Stay covered.

Chapter 5 Childhood Sexual Abuse

If you are still asking why God allows terrible things to happen especially to children please hear this truth.

Before sin entered the world, everything God created was pure and good. The devil's mission has always been to twist and corrupt what God made beautiful.

God gave us plants for healing and nourishment; the devil turned many of them into addiction.
God gave us currency for stewardship and generosity; the devil turned it into greed and debt.
God designed sex as a sacred bond between husband and wife; the devil distorted it through lust, pornography, and abuse.
God anointed certain people with healing hands; the devil convinced some to use that same gift to harm others.

Even the Bible our guide for truth has been misused by those who treat it like a spell book rather than the living Word of God.

Remember: the devil was God's creation, a magnificent angel. He was meant to serve and glorify God but chose rebellion instead. The gifts he once had are now used for destruction. Everything God loves, the devil hates.

He loves confusion, division, and pain.
He loves broken homes, sickness, addiction, and unforgiveness.
So, naturally, he *hates* children because they represent innocence and purity.

Children are the closest reflection of innocence on earth. That is why the devil seeks to corrupt them early: to steal their innocence, to silence their voices, and to plant seeds of pain that grow into bitterness and unbelief.

This is why so many adults who were hurt as children struggle to forgive. The devil's goal is to wound you so deeply that you never heal so that you live your entire life angry at God, unable to walk in your calling.

But God's goal is the opposite: to heal you, free you, and use your story to save others.

When we refuse to forgive, that pain transforms into bitterness, fear, addiction, self-sabotage, and broken relationships. Unforgiveness keeps us chained to the very people who hurt us. It robs us of peace and purpose.

Forgiveness doesn't excuse what happened it releases you from it. You cannot fully become who God designed you to be if you remain bound by what someone did to you.

You may never receive an apology.
You may never hear the words "I'm sorry."
But God saw everything. He knows. And His justice is perfect.

Every child who was emotionally, physically, spiritually, or sexually abused myself included is seen by God. He intervenes in ways we may not understand. In time, He transforms our pain into purpose.

Many of us believe no one else could possibly understand what we've endured. But Scripture reminds us: *"There is nothing new under the sun."* (Ecclesiastes 1:9) You are not alone, and your struggle is not unique to you. That means your healing is possible.

God did not create your suffering. The devil hates your destiny, and he targeted you early because he saw the calling over your life.

Your pain sharpened your discernment. Many survivors can now sense darkness in others. I can feel the presence of a predatory spirit even when I have no proof, and that awareness, is a gift from God. It allows me to pray, to intercede, and to protect.

If you ever feel uneasy around someone who works with or cares for children, do not ignore that feeling. Trust your discernment. Pray immediately.

I've seen the spirit of predation in people others would never suspect men, women, even those considered beautiful or highly respected. Evil hides behind charm.

Always pray before allowing anyone access to children, especially those eager to "help" without pay. Genuine servants exist, but discernment is vital.

Many who were molested as children have been equipped with the spiritual ability to recognize and confront that same evil before it harms someone else. Use that gift through prayer and intercession.

Pray for *all* children girls and boys alike. Society often overlooks the silent pain of boys who were violated and they are taught to hide it. Pray also for children with special needs who cannot easily speak for themselves.

Remember: **prayer and worship are our greatest weapons.**

Being angry with God because of something the devil did, is the same thing as being angry at someone's father, because their son robbed a bank!! It makes no sense!!!!!

There are PLENTY OF US, that have children who display behaviors, that are completely OPPOSITE of how we raised them!

Through forgiveness, intercession, and the power of Jesus Christ, every curse of abuse can be broken. God can restore innocence, peace, and strength where trauma once lived.

Chapter 6 Tell God How You Feel

This chapter is about the importance of having an *honest* relationship with God.
It's time to stop hiding how you really feel.

Take off the mask of perfection. Remove the guilt and fear. Be completely transparent with our Creator.

Tell God exactly how you feel, respectfully, but honestly.

The beautiful thing about this truth is that God already knows.
Jeremiah 1:5 says, *"Before I formed you in the womb, I knew you."*
He already knows your heart every thought, every frustration, every wound.

And you would be surprised by the peace and revelation that comes when you finally express your feelings directly to Him.

Don't give God a watered-down version of your emotions. Don't pray vague prayers out of politeness or fear. He doesn't need a rehearsed speech; He wants the real you.

Say it plainly:

"God, I am frustrated. I am hurt. I am angry. I don't understand why my life looks like this when I've tried so hard to do everything right."

That is not rebellion that's honesty.

Tell Him,

"God, I've been fasting. I've been praying. I've been anointing my home, my children, my spouse. I've been forgiving people who hurt me. I've been mindful of what I eat, what I watch, and how I live yet my life still feels like chaos."

Ask Him the question you've been holding back:

"Why isn't my life working out when I'm doing everything You asked me to do?"

Sometimes God's answer is simple: **"It's coming."**
Other times, His response is, **"I'm not giving you what you're asking for because it would bring problems you're not prepared to handle."**
And sometimes His answer is, **"I have something better for you."**

But there's another answer we rarely want to hear the one that convicts us most deeply.

Sometimes God says:

"You think you've been doing everything right, but I see what others don't."

He might remind you:

"I see the secret addiction you haven't surrendered. I see the person you still haven't forgiven. I see the gossip in your conversations, the pride in your heart, the compromise at your job. I see the lies you told years ago that you never corrected."

You might attend Church faithfully, tithe regularly, and serve in Ministry but still be living in quiet disobedience.

God might say:

"You treat Me like a job you can clock out from. You worship Me on Sunday but feed your spirit with ungodly things during the week. You say you love Me, but you fear your boss more than you fear Me. You obey the world faster than you obey My Word."

That truth stings, but it's freeing. Because conviction is the beginning of transformation.

When you come before God honestly not as a "perfect Christian" but as a humble child who's hurting He will meet you there.

He won't reject your honesty.
He won't condemn your questions.
He will embrace your truth and exchange your anger for peace.

You can tell God everything. There is nothing He hasn't seen, nothing He can't handle, and nothing He can't heal.

Honesty doesn't drive Him away, it draws Him closer.

Chapter 7 Real vs Lukewarm

Some of us think we are Christians when, in reality, we are **lukewarm**.

You might be asking, *"What's the difference between a real Christian and a lukewarm Christian?"*
The difference is commitment. The difference is consistency. The difference is character when no one is watching.

A **real Christian** worships God every day not just on Sunday.
A real Christian, though not perfect, strives every moment to be Christlike.
A real Christian does the right thing even when it's uncomfortable or unseen.
A real Christian is humble, not boastful, and carries such a strong presence of the Holy Spirit that even unbelievers can sense that something about them is different.

Now let's talk about **lukewarm Christians.**

Lukewarm Christians are holy only on Sundays.
From Monday to Saturday, you wouldn't know they belong to God.
They are afraid to praise God publicly if the people around them don't believe.
They avoid talking about Jesus for fear of offending others.
They rely on their pastors to interpret the Bible instead of studying it for themselves.
They think that giving time or money to the Church alone, guarantees heaven.

Lukewarm Christians are more concerned with their **image** than their **relationship** with God.

Have you ever noticed that in Churches where the congregation is wealthy, there's often less open worship? People sit quietly, afraid to shout "Hallelujah" because they don't want to appear emotional. Yet in less affluent congregations, people shout, dance, cry, and worship freely because they remember where God brought them from.

That difference is heart posture.

When people start getting the money, success, or comfort they prayed for, many forget *who* blessed them in the first place. They become too refined to praise, too educated to shout, too poised to lift their hands.

That is lukewarm.

Lukewarm Christians also avoid accountability. They don't like to be corrected and refuse to correct others. They pick and choose which parts of the Bible to follow, embracing only verses that comfort them while ignoring those that convict them.

They might say things like "Follow your heart," believing it's biblical. But the Bible actually says the opposite:

"The heart is deceitful above all things and desperately wicked." (Jeremiah 17:9)

This is why studying the Word personally, is so important. Hosea 4:6 warns, *"My people are destroyed for lack of knowledge."*

If we depend entirely on others to tell us what God's Word says, we become spiritually lazy.
It's okay to take time even years to truly understand a

single book of the Bible.
Depth is more powerful than speed.

Lukewarm Christians also believe their good deeds erase their sins. But works alone don't save anyone.

They may serve, donate, or volunteer yet still gossip, lie, envy, and compromise when tempted.
They are quick to praise publicly but slow to repent privately.
They can't stand being corrected by someone walking in truth.

Meanwhile, **real Christians** welcome correction, because they know it leads to growth.

So ask yourself today:
Am I living as a real Christian, or a lukewarm one?
Do I worship God when no one's watching?
Do I obey Him even when it costs me?
Do I read His Word for myself, or only hear about it from others?

Jesus said in Revelation 3:16,

"Because you are lukewarm neither hot nor cold I am about to spit you out of my mouth."

That is a sobering truth.

You cannot serve two masters. You cannot live halfway for God.

Be bold. Be steadfast. Be all in.

Chapter 8 The Consequences

Leaving the presence of God because you're angry, heartbroken, or bitter is **one of the most dangerous things you could ever do.**

When people get angry with God, they often start to question His existence.
They stop going to Church.
They stop reading the Bible.
They cut off their relationship with Him completely.

But let me ask you this:
When you're angry at a friend, do you immediately end the friendship forever?
When your pet misbehaves, do you take it to the shelter and give it away?
When you argue with a loved one, do you stop loving them completely?

Most of us don't do that.
Yet many people abandon God because of disappointment as if walking away from Him will fix the pain inside.

It won't.

When you separate yourself from God, you open the door for the enemy to enter your life.
The devil thrives in the absence of divine covering.
If you remove God's protection, you invite destruction emotionally, mentally, spiritually, financially, and even physically.

There are people right now whose lives are falling apart simply because they made the choice to distance themselves from God.

Please don't become one of them.

I wrote this book because I understand how you feel. I've been there.
I wrote this because I love you even if we've never met.
I want you to know that you are seen, that your pain is valid, and that you are not alone.

You are not the only person who has ever been angry with God.
And just like there's light at the end of every tunnel, there is light at the end of this one, too.

That light is called **redemption.**

Imagine this:
You cut God out of your life because you didn't get what you wanted.
You stopped praying, fasting, or believing.
And in that void, the devil moves in not to comfort you, but to destroy you.

He destroys peace.
He destroys relationships.
He destroys health.
And ultimately, he destroys eternal life.

All because you couldn't wait on God.

Maybe you've been praying for a specific job something that pays well and brings prestige but God keeps closing doors. What if it's because He's called you to build your own business, one that could bless countless people and bring you greater abundance than you ever imagined?

Maybe you've been praying for a romantic relationship that hasn't worked out. You're angry because the person you love doesn't love you back. But what if God is protecting you from someone too self-centered to care for you when you're old, sick, or struggling and preparing someone better who will love you unconditionally?

Maybe you're angry because you were abused, not realizing that once you heal, your story could help thousands find deliverance. Maybe your pain will become a bestselling book that builds generational wealth and brings freedom to others who thought they were alone.

Maybe your struggle isn't punishment maybe it's purpose.

So many of us waste our pain by refusing to heal, when that pain was designed to elevate us.

You might be praying for something small when God has something *massive* waiting.

You're praying for an assistant manager position but God destined you to be a CEO.
You're praying for a child but God has appointed you to rescue and raise a foster child who will one day change the world.
You're praying for a nicer apartment but God wants to make you a homeowner.

But He can't give you these things until your heart is ready to handle them.

We often confuse waiting with punishment.
But waiting is God's classroom. It's where faith is refined, strength is built, and destiny is shaped.

If you're angry about your living situation maybe you don't like your home, your neighborhood, or the fact that you have to share a space with family. Take a moment to be grateful.

You have a roof. You have running water. You have electricity.
There are people all over the world who have none of those things.

Gratitude keeps your heart open for blessing.
Ingratitude shuts the door.

The Bible says, *"Faith without works is dead."* (James 2:17)
So don't just pray take action.
If you want change, start building. If you want a breakthrough, plant seeds.

But above all, don't turn your back on God.

Walking away from Him won't speed up your blessing it will delay it even further.

Please, don't allow your soul to perish because you refused to wait.

Stay faithful.
Stay patient.
Stay under God's covering.

Because leaving His presence doesn't punish Him it only leaves *you* exposed.

Chapter 9 God is NOT Your Personal Genie

Have you ever been to a barbecue, a party, or a club where there was a DJ playing music?
There were times in my past when I would go to lounges or events and ask the DJ to play a specific song.
Sometimes, I would even slip them a little money and say, "Can you please play this next?"

The DJ would usually smile and say, *"I got you."*

So naturally, I expected my song to come on within the next two or three songs.
But hours would pass 9 p.m., 10 p.m., 11 p.m. and my song still hadn't played.

By 11:15, I'd be frustrated. *"I asked him early! I even tipped him! Why hasn't he played my song yet?"*

But what I didn't realize at the time was that the DJ had a plan.
I wasn't the only person who made a request. Other people had asked for songs too and many had also paid.

The DJ knew something I didn't know: timing.

He knew which songs to play early and which ones to save for later, based on the energy in the room. He knew when the crowd would respond best. If he played everything too soon, the energy would die too fast.

He had a vision a rhythm and he was going to stick to it.

So even though I was impatient, the DJ was never late. My request wasn't forgotten; it was just waiting for the *right time.*

We treat **God** the exact same way.

We pray for something and expect it to happen immediately as if we've just tipped heaven's DJ to play our song next.

We think, *"God, I prayed this morning, so by tonight, it should be done."*
Or, *"God, I've been good all week. I deserve my blessing now."*

But God doesn't operate on our schedule.
He's not moved by our impatience.
He's not pressured by our deadlines.

He has divine timing.

Just like the DJ, He knows what songs what blessings belong in which part of your life's playlist.
And if He plays something too early, it might ruin the entire rhythm of your destiny.

That's why we must learn to trust His timing even when we're tired of waiting.

God is not your personal genie.

You can't rub a lamp, make a wish, and expect Him to appear with a checklist.

And thank God for that!
Because if He were a genie, He wouldn't hold you

accountable for your choices.
He wouldn't care about your eternal soul only your temporary satisfaction.

But God isn't interested in giving you three wishes.
He's interested in giving you *everlasting life*.

I've never heard of a genie dying on the cross for me.
I've never heard of a genie offering unconditional forgiveness, peace, and redemption.

A genie can only grant your requests not heal your soul.
God, on the other hand, transforms your heart before granting your desires.

So if you're waiting on God and wondering why your "song" hasn't played yet, remember: He's working according to the rhythm of eternity, not the clock of impatience.

Maybe He's building your character before your blessing.
Maybe He's testing your faith before your promotion.
Maybe He's protecting you from something that looks good but could destroy you.

And sometimes, He's just saying, *"Not yet, My child the crowd isn't ready, and neither are you."*

If you can wait on a DJ to play your favorite song…
If you can wait months for a promotion…
If you can wait years for someone to love you back…

Then surely, you can wait on God the same God who sacrificed His Son for you.

Trust His plan.
Trust His playlist.
Because when your song finally plays, it will be worth every moment you waited.

Chapter 10 Don't be Weak!

As long as you are living and breathing, the enemy **will** try to attack you.
That is a guarantee.

Blaming God is a sign of weakness and **you are not weak.**

In this life, you must fight.
As long as you are a child of light, the darkness will always try to pull you down.

And when you begin to blame God, it's a sign that the devil has started working in your mind.
He attacks your thoughts first.

Once he gets control of your thoughts, everything else begins to crumble.

His process is strategic. It often looks like this:

1. You become **angry with God.**
2. You begin to **doubt God.**
3. You stop **fearing God.**
4. You **end your relationship** with Him.
5. You start **worshiping other idols** people, possessions, relationships, or substances.
6. You begin to **live a sinful life.**
7. Finally, the **devil destroys your life.**

And this cycle continues until death unless you break it through repentance and submission to God.

This is the cycle:

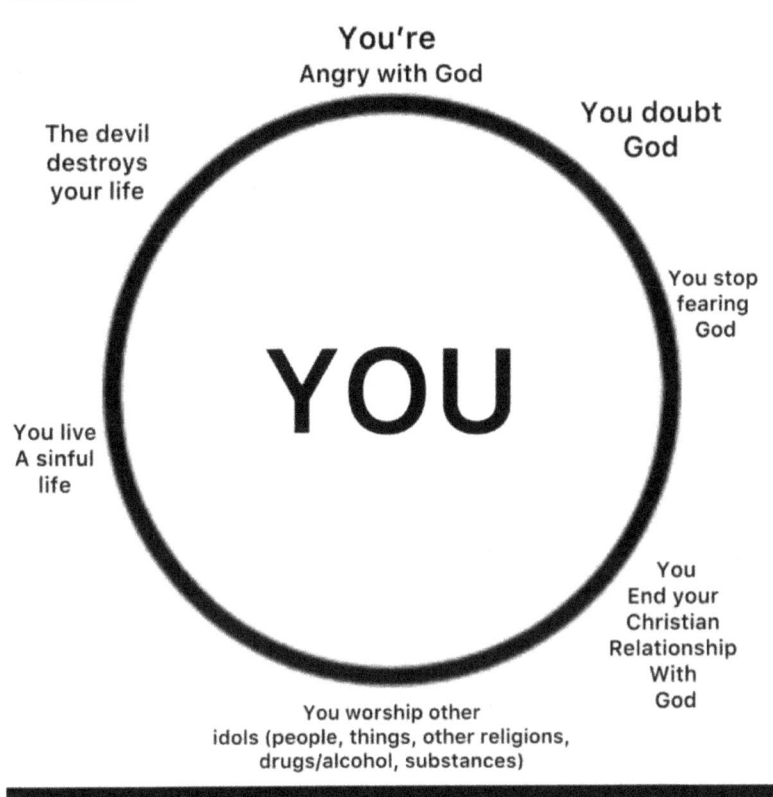

When you stop fearing God, you start fearing everything else.
Without reverence for Him, your spirit becomes vulnerable afraid of people, circumstances, and problems.

But when you **fear God alone**, you have no fear left for anything or anyone else.

That's the secret of spiritual strength.

The devil doesn't know what to do with a believer who praises God through pain.

So when life hurts, **confuse him.**

When friendships end, say:

"Thank You, Lord!"

When you lose a job, say:

"Thank You, Lord!"

When your finances drop, say:

"Thank You, Lord!"

When health issues arise, say it again:

"Thank You, Lord!"

Every time you thank God in the middle of your storm, the devil becomes more frustrated because you're proving that no weapon formed against you shall prosper.

Praising God through pain breaks hell's strategy.
It's the most powerful act of defiance against darkness.

So when the devil attacks your mind, your peace, or your faith **don't be weak.**
Stand firm. Speak life. Worship louder.

Because when you refuse to surrender your praise, you remind the enemy that you belong to a victorious God.

And no demon, lie, or situation can change that truth.

Chapter 11 The Bottom Line

The bottom line is this:
Sometimes, God's answer to your prayer is simply **"No."**

God is not going to say yes to everything you ask for.

Many of us have been conditioned by **prosperity preaching,** the belief that if we tithe, pray, attend Church, and do "all the right things," God will automatically say yes to every request.

That is not biblical truth.

Prosperity preachers often tell you that your "breakthrough is coming," that "this is your season," or that "God is about to do wonders in your life."

But the reality is not every season is a season of breakthrough.
Sometimes, it's a season of **testing, pruning, suffering, or stillness.**

There are seasons when God is silent because He's strengthening your spirit.
There are seasons when the answer is "no" because the blessing you're praying for would destroy you.

If your relationship with God is based only on what He gives you, then it's not a relationship it's a transaction.

Serving God so He'll "do something for you" is not faith; it's manipulation.
And God cannot be manipulated.

Do not let false prophets deceive you.
They sound good because they promise constant blessings without correction.
But they rarely talk about repentance, accountability, or discipline.

If all you ever hear is "God will bless you" and never "God will refine you," then you're not hearing the full truth.

Real pastors teach the whole gospel both grace **and** growth, blessing **and** obedience.

Be wary of preachers who stand in pulpits wearing $10,000 suits, driving luxury cars, and boasting of their prosperity while their congregation waits at the bus stop.

If money equaled Holiness, then only the rich would be blessed but that's not what Scripture teaches.

Matthew 5:5 says,

"Blessed are the meek, for they shall inherit the earth."

Humility, not wealth, is what moves the heart of God.

You might be praying for a promotion or a "better" job and feel overlooked but maybe this season isn't about advancement.
Maybe it's about humility.

Who decided that jobs like janitors, maids, or servers were beneath anyone?
Society did, not God.

It's those same jobs that support families, keep communities running, and teach the discipline of hard work.

Even Jesus' earthly father, **Joseph**, was a carpenter a humble trade.
And Jesus Himself didn't walk the earth draped in gold or luxury.

He walked in simplicity and power, not in wealth and pride.

So don't despise small beginnings or humble seasons.
They are often the very places where God trains you for your greatest calling.

Here's the bottom line again:
Sometimes, **God's "no" is mercy.**
Sometimes, **His silence is protection.**
And sometimes, **His delay is preparation.**

Don't measure your faith by what you've received.
Measure it by what you've survived, what you've learned, and how steadfast you remain when Heaven is quiet.

God doesn't owe us constant comfort He offers us eternal life.
And that is the greatest "yes" we could ever receive.

Chapter 12 Stay Focused

Not getting what you want whether immediately or even years later is **not** a reason to lose focus.

Sometimes, we pray for things and expect God to answer within days or weeks. But what if His timeline isn't measured in minutes or months? What if it's measured in maturity?

There are things we ask for that we're simply **not ready for yet.**
If we were ready, we would already have them.

So instead of asking, *"Why hasn't God given me this yet?"* Start asking, *"What is God preparing me for, and what is He still preparing **in** me?"*

God's delay is often His way of building your strength and refining your heart so you can handle what's coming.

If you feel blocked or stagnant, ask yourself:
Is there someone I still need to forgive?
Is there pride or bitterness I haven't released?
Am I holding onto habits or relationships that God asked me to let go of?

These are the things that quietly block blessings.

Sometimes, God won't open a new door until we close the wrong one.
Sometimes, we delay our own progress by clinging to what He's already asked us to surrender.

Lack of money is not a reason to give up.
Your current situation is not your final destination.

Many successful people once had nothing.
Some lived in cars, others lost everything yet they didn't quit.

They persisted.
They trusted.
They believed that every "no" was leading to the right "yes."

The same equation applies to you:
God + Persistence = Ultimate Success.

It is impossible to walk in victory if you constantly see yourself as a victim.

Faith and self-pity cannot occupy the same space.

You cannot be focused on your purpose while being fixated on your pain.

Never take your eyes off God.

When He is at the center of your focus, everything else aligns even when life feels chaotic.

God's presence in your situation protects you in ways you may never see. He blocks accidents you didn't know were coming, delays you from meetings that would have hurt you, and reroutes you away from people meant to destroy your peace.

So when things don't go your way, stop and thank Him.
His "no" is often divine protection.

Whenever you feel angry, admit it respectfully.
Be honest with God about your emotions, but never disconnect from Him.

Write down what you're feeling.
Keep a journal where you list your frustrations and then your blessings side by side. You'll often find that what you *have* outweighs what you *lack*.

And when you look back, you'll realize that everything you thought was delayed was actually being prepared.

Stay focused.

God will give you everything He has designed for your life not a moment too soon and not a moment too late.

As long as you keep following Him, protection, success, and abundance will follow you.

Never forget this: every time you're tempted to give up, you are often closer to your breakthrough than you realize.

Don't quit now.
Don't lose focus.
Don't stop believing.

Because the same God who began a good work in you, will be faithful to complete it.

Thank You

Thank you for taking the time to read this book.
Your time matters, and I don't take it for granted.

If you would like prayer or would like to schedule a life-coaching session, you can reach me at:
✉ thelifecoachjimmy@gmail.com

I love you.
I believe in you.
And I am grateful for you.

Stay strong, stay faithful and never stop talking to God.

www.ingramcontent.com/pod-product-compliance
Lightning Source LLC
Chambersburg PA
CBHW050728010526
44107CB00009B/780